DON'T
BOW

DANIEL 3:17-18

DON'T BOW

Standing against the Idols of Our Generation

DeMarquis R. Battle

BATTLE
LEADERSHIP GROUP LLC

BATTLE 4 CHRIST PUBLISHING, LLC

Don't Bow
Standing against the Idols of Our Generation

Copyright © 2013 by DeMarquis R. Battle

Published by Battle 4 Christ Publishing, LLC
P.O. Box 81189
Lansing, MI 48908

Printed in the United States of America
ISBN: 978-0615860947

Learn more information about:
www.battleleadershipgroup.com

ACKNOWLEDGMENTS

There are so many people that I would like to acknowledge in writing this book. I have a special spot for my immediate family in the dedication but I would like to highlight a few individuals now. I first want to acknowledge Jesus Christ for saving my life. I was on a path to destruction but He rescued my heart. I endeavor to live each day for Him and through my life reach others to come into relationship with the almighty God.

I want to acknowledge my mother who has always believed in me. Mom I want to say thank you for all of the long talks and the words of wisdom. I remember our talks about scripture, history, and politics. No matter the conversation you always listened. You supported me in everything I got involved in. I also want to thank you for instilling Christian values into me at a young age. You worked very hard to raise me and I appreciate all you have done.

I want to acknowledge my Dad who has become one of my closest friends. I also thank you for the long talks and lectures that were packed with wisdom, laughter, serious undertones, and love. You have always treated me like a man and taught me what hard work looks like. I am forever grateful. I also want to acknowledge my step-mother for loving and believing in me. You are a beautiful and caring person and I am better for having you in my life.

I want to acknowledge my older sister Queayna. Thank you Que for always being there for me. You were my defender and protector. You were the vehicle that helped me reach the starting point of my destiny as a minister of the Gospel. Without your love and support I would not be here right now.

I want to thank all of my family members that supported and believed in me. From my Grandma Agnew who urged me to go up for prayer to get saved every Sunday as a child. To my Grandfather Agnew who taught me through his life to never be ashamed of the Gospel of Jesus Christ. He always had a praise on his lips.

To my Grandma and Grandpa Battle who taught me through their lives a lesson of love and family. I want to acknowledge my younger siblings Randy, Raven, and my baby brother TaVeon. Thank you for allowing me to be a big brother. You all pushed me to be an example, and challenged me to lay a foundation for our families. To the aunts and uncles who prayed for me continually. I am forever thankful.

I want to acknowledge my spiritual father and mother, Pastors Sean and Tayana Holland. Pastor, you sowed the "Don't Bow" message into my spirit at a time when I doubted my calling. You both believed in me and cheered me on to be the best husband, father, and preacher I could be. Without your leadership and guidance I could not be in the place I am today.

I want to acknowledge my youth groups Tri-C and IMPACT. Each and every one of you all inspired me to write this book. I cannot wait to see you all become the world changers I know God has created you all to be! I want to thank my church family, The Epicenter of Worship for their support. There are many of you that prayed for me and my wife and we are forever grateful. There are so many others that have impacted my life in a positive way from high school teachers and coaches to college and seminary professors. From the bottom of my heart I acknowledge and thank you all.

Sincerely,

DeMarquis R. Battle

DEDICATION

I dedicate this book to two of the most special individuals in my life, my wife and son. Raynika, throughout my journey in ministry you have been there as my greatest supporter. I truly believe that you are God sent. At my mountaintops you were with me. At my valley lows you were still with me. You have been there through all of my creative ideas and my midnight dreams. For all of the car side chats we had, you were always willing to give a smile, a small dose of reality, and a heart full of faith. I am forever grateful to you and I love you.

Now to my little man Justus. You are my motivation to continue pushing forward. You have been such a blessing to me words cannot fully explain. You make me laugh and smile at your silliness. You amaze me with your talent and your caring heart even at a toddler's age. There is no doubt that you will be the leader that God has destined for you to be. I pray that this book will be ready for you to read when the time is right and that you will never bow down to the images and idols that will be present in your time.

I love you guys!

Sincerely,

Your Husband and Father

DeMarquis R. Battle

CONTENTS

INTRODUCTION

We are in a war! Please don't mistake the confrontation between two forces as anything less. The world has released its warfare sound and our generation has unlimited access to it. What is this sound? It is the sound produced by man-made idols.

These idols that are prevalent in the music and entertainment industries influence our youth to pattern their lives after them. Our youth are forced knowingly and unknowingly to bow down to an unrighteous societal standard, which in turn causes a compromise of their faith. Materialism, popularity, and acceptance have become the object of our generation's affection. This is the world's message and this is their sound.

Still you have a choice. God has given you a will, and with it you can determine what enters into your heart. You can be subject to the popular yet destructive sounds and visuals or you can take a righteous stand.

You can usher in the sound of intense praise as a generation of worshipers. You can exhibit the courage of Daniel, the strength of Moses, and the character of our Christ. You can change the culture of our nation by standing up for the name of Jesus.

So again, there is a war going on. Will you bow down to the idols that our young people face daily or will you stand against it and reflect the image of Christ in the earth? Jesus is calling us to make the sound of worship and reveal His glory. He is calling us to live an uncompromised life that will be a testimony to many. Listen to these words that echoed in my heart when Jesus got a hold of it. DON'T BOW!

Don't Bow
Standing against the Idols of Our Generation

1

What are Images and Idols?

I asked myself the same question when God began to speak to me about my life and the generation of which I am apart. From a Biblical perspective I knew what images and idols were. Growing up in the church, every child was taught the Ten Commandments repetitively and with precision, as if our lives depended on them. I thank God for every Sunday school teacher who invested in the lives of little children with something as simple as Christian nursery rhymes. The foundation of God's word that was laid for me and countless others are irreplaceable. The Bible is clear on the Lord's stance on idols and idol worship.

Exodus 20:3-4 describes:

- "You shall have no other gods before me. You shall not make for yourself a carved image, or any likeness of anything that is in heaven above, or that is in the earth beneath, or that is in the water under the earth."

Idol worship is a very serious offense to God. Think of all the commands the Lord gave to the Israelites. The Lord decides to deal first with false gods, images, and idol worship. The reason it is so troubling to God is because it can put you in a place of total separation from Him and affect your understanding of who He is. The Israelites put their trust in idols because of its familiarity in prior situations and because of the idol's popularity in the land they would inhabit. God doesn't want you to depend on anything other than Him. Idol worship can literally destroy you spiritually and emotionally.

Even with the understanding that God doesn't want any false gods before Him, I had not yet brought this into my modern day context. The first thing that comes to mind was a golden animal statue like a calf, or a large Buddha replica that weighed a ton and sat still gathering dust in someone's display case. In fact my grandmother had one of these images in her living room for years. She didn't worship the idol that plagued her home but it was used as a show piece more than anything else. Little did I know several years later I would be called by God as a minister of His Gospel and that I was about to gain revelation of the images and idols that don't sit still in showcases, but are alive in the secret places of our hearts.

In order to truly gain an understanding of what this generation is faced with regarding images and idols there has to be a working definition for both terms. First there is an **IMAGE**. This is defined as a representation of a person, animal, or any other object; that is produced through a picture, a sculpture, or visible in any other format. A second definition says that it is a representation in the mind, a conception, or idea. So literally an image could be anything you could imagine. It is shaped by someone's hands, both physically and spiritually to send a particular message.

Images are powerful. They can fill your mind and send messages that God did not intend for you to receive. Our generation is infatuated with images through the internet and on social media. Ask yourself this question. What images are being feed to my spirit on a daily basis that will undoubtedly tear me down and put a false understanding of my identity and purpose within my heart? The answer might surprise you.

Now I will highlight an **IDOL**. This is defined as an image representing a deity that is worshiped religiously. It is any person or thing who is highly regarded, who is worshiped, adored and whose followers are devoted to them blindly. These two definitions separately are powerful, but together their meanings are amplified.

The revelation that God gave me concerning the two definitions and how they impact today's generation was amazing. As an example I ask that you consider any of today's musical talent search programs on television. For the last decade America has been captivated by the successes and failures of these contestants as they try to make the "big time" in the music and entertainment industry. Many have spent hours in line waiting for an opportunity to prove their worth. Displaying their gift, each contestant stands before a panel of celebrity judges who holds the contestants fate in their hands. Each individual selects a well-crafted song that is performed with limited time to do nothing more than create a buzz of intrigue in the judges minds. In an instance your vocal ability can be held in high regard or just average compared to the masses. One by one the contestant hopes to be granted a ticket to the next round of auditions. Dreams are birthed through each session that the contestant goes through. The ultimate goal is to make the live show which will bring them steps closer to busting through the industry wall and into idol status.

Picture one contestant, a young girl comes with a certain style, a specific personality and demeanor. She comes in with an **IMAGE**. The judge who stands as a symbol of the world takes that contestant and determines that her image will not be suitable for the industry because it is too safe. News flash, the world doesn't want conservative images but it desires to be as edgy and sexual as possible. The enemy rather a whole generation of young people fair on the side of edginess and compromise than to exhibit conservative values. Sure you may be able to hold on to your image for a season but the expectation is that you will give up who you are

3

for what you can become in the world. This is just another sign of the moral decay our nation is experiencing. Our next generation leaders are being pimped by secularism.

After an image has been identified the industry begins to shape the participant into the **IDOL** that will appeal to the nation. It doesn't take a rocket scientist to know what image appeals to the masses in today's society. Once this has occurred they will slowly strip the contestant of all they have been brought to know, everything they have learned, their moral stance and biblical beliefs and bring them into an arena of **IDOL** fame. They are now lifted up as an idol for worship in our generation. This should not be anything new to anyone who has been watching what the industry has been feeding our generation. The formula has been consistent for some time now. Think back to some of the famous child television and movie stars. They all came into the industry with their innocence and purity only to be stripped gradually of that identity and eventually infused into the image that binds the hearts of our young men and woman into idol worship!

Thousands of young people have a yearning to use the talent that God has given them, not knowing that the world is looking to rob them of that gift which is meant to glorify God. Our enemy is hungry to corrupt the talent that God has released into your hands. A few things can happen from this corruption. The enemy will either lift you up as an idol or flash before you the wealth of this world so that you become an idol worshipper seeking the status of men. The difference between idol worship 20 years ago and today is access. We have so many opportunities to be sucked into the system of idol worship it is ridiculous. Perception is reality and for hundreds and thousands of teenagers around the country what they see is reality to them. They have accepted these lies as truth.

All of a sudden one day it all made sense. Before I received the love of God and accepted Jesus as my lord and savior I had a completely different life. I had a certain mindset, the same type of thinking many of the young people I encounter have today. Success to me was defined by the amount of cash I had or the amount that I would eventually obtain. My swag was determined by the type of car I would drive. My level of influence was impacted by the ungodly relationships I would form and the power I would receive. All of these desires were lustful. What this meant was that the things I couldn't afford nor needed, I wanted them badly. I wanted them for two reasons. The first was to be admired like an Idol. I wanted people to respect, love, and worship me. Before you become self-righteous and look down on my statement just think about it, who didn't want to be the coolest guy or girl around? Who didn't want to be admired? Who wouldn't want to feel powerful and successful among their peers?

The second reason was fear that I would never come into something special. Most of the people I knew have never achieved a status of fame. For many young people who are struggling with their identity, they seem to view wealth and power like a fairytale. They follow the success stories of celebrities with child-like faith, wishing it were them while yet ignoring the realities of life. This doesn't mean you can't have dreams of doing great things but it does indicate a level of ignorance that is upon our generation. For me this type of mindset was produced out of a supposed lack that I had and a feeling of inadequacy as a young African-American teenager.

Why did I think like this? The answer is now clear to me and I pray it becomes clearer to you. What is portrayed before you is the enemy's plan for you to chase after and to become a participant of idol worship. Many of today's entertainers, actors, and models were normal talented individuals like you and I. Many of them have been raised in Christian homes and the anointing and favor of God was on their lives. This is not to say that an individual cannot seek to become successful in any of the domains of society, or that their hard work is not honorable. The issue is what one has to

5

do to get into the position of fame and fortune. Will you compromise your relationship with Jesus for success? Will you ignore Jesus to remain popular and avoid persecution from your peers because of your faith?

Instead of seeking after the will of God for your life and glorifying Him with the gifts He gave you, the enemy wants you to bow down to the images and idols that are prevalent in our world right now and give him all the praise. Who are the idols of our generation that I am referring to? They can be a number of different individuals. I challenge you to take out a pen and a piece of paper. In five minutes write down the different areas of entertainment. Include the various genres of music you listen to, the various movies that you watch and the actors who star in those roles, even the famous athletes that you like. I guarantee that more than half of those individuals you list on your paper are a modern day idol to our generation. The artists that made the cut of your idol list more than likely portray images of money, sex, and power. The movie star who wears certain clothes, eats at particular restaurants, practices a specific diet and entertains a certain religion has gained power to influence a generation. Even some of our most beloved athletes have impacted our stance on modern day issues and affect our worship. The enemy knows that these celebrities have influence and with that influence have power to shift a generation's focus and desire.

These various images are so easily accessible all you would have to do is turn on your television for 10 seconds or boot up your computer and visit any website, and instantly suggestive ads will appear before your eyes. Spam will be all over the place with provocative images of men and women. An average commercial runs 15-30 seconds with a 2-3 minute window before the program you are watching comes back on. Imagine within that time frame the amount of messages that have been sent to your mind regarding images and idols. This is the type of warfare our generation is under. It is a consistent onslaught of images that bring us further away from God's presence and purpose for our lives.

Many of the youth groups that I have ministered to are interested in knowing if their favorite artist is in a secret society or some type of occult activity. This would be the kind of underground group that is fueled by idol worship. Based upon our definitions I would say a majority of them are. Many of these beloved individuals have immersed themselves into unhealthy activity that is detrimental to their lives, and if mimicked by our youth will bring about even greater destruction to this generation! Conspiracy theories aside, you can look at secular entertainment at the base level and see the darkness these artists are involved in. It gives you a clearer picture of what we as a nation are dealing with. Does what I see or hear bring me closer to the presence of God or not? The Bible instructs us to flee from sin. As a young man and representative of this generation I stand on that command.

The world wants you to see these artists basking in riches and appearing happy with their lives. We see music videos of rappers and singers with bottles of alcohol and smoking marijuana. We see them dancing to the latest hit single and looking entertained in that atmosphere. On the outside that may very well be the case. Their flesh is entertained but deep within deception has wrapped itself around their heart and has inserted destructive images and idols into it. Many of these artists wear clothing that suggests their allegiance to darkness yet we ignore this symbolism. To the average eye none of this matters because it is just an art-form, and it should not be taken literally. Sometimes one can be so blind that they are not in a position to believe. The world wants you to see these individuals and the "*get rich or die trying*" success story. Those who desire to see a generation swallowed up and led astray want things to appear like one big party.

One of the more popular sayings today in the hip-hop community and among youth throughout America is the term

"YOLO", which means "You Only Live Once". In this mantra you are encouraged to do whatever you want to do with the life you have been given. Isn't this an interesting motto to live by? So many young people take this saying from famous rappers in the music industry and follow after their pattern not really understanding the method behind the madness. Leaders of the occult world have a similar saying which is to "Do as thou wilt". If our young people understood that their life is not their own but they are to live for Christ maybe their actions would be different. The world has tried its best to make living for Jesus seem like some sort of chore or something that is not cool or satisfying. This can be no further from the truth. It is more fulfilling to live for Jesus Christ than it is to enjoy sin for a season and live a life of false fulfillment.

The second saying that is popular today is "Turn Up." This would imply turning up the intensity of your attitude or demeanor in preparation of a party or outing. To turn up is to literally increase your engagement in any activity especially parties and the use of alcohol and or drugs. I know what most of you are thinking. "It's not that deep," or "We are just saying it, but not really trying to do all that stuff." Well, the Bible clearly has a stand against turning up. Romans 13:13 states the following:

- Because we belong to the day, we must live decent lives for all to see. Don't participate in the darkness of wild parties and drunkenness, or in sexual promiscuity and immoral living, or in quarreling and jealousy (*New Living Translation, 2008*).

The phrase does have some harmless meaning to it, but in most cases it describes a desire for drunkenness and lustful interaction. These are the images that our generation see and hear and are influenced by. Idols give off the appearance that if you hustle hard the world is yours for the taking. You do reap what you sow. Many of our young people are tricked into sowing their lives to this lifestyle but in the end they only reap a harvest of spiritual destruction. The Bible is clear regarding the desire of worldly things. In Mark 8:36 it states:

- "For what does it profit a man to gain the whole world and forfeit his soul?"

My suggestion is not to be fooled by what you see. Let the light of God illuminate the secret place of your heart and expose the plan of the enemy. At the end of the day sin is looking to come and bind you up. It desires to bring you in by the images and idols of entertainment. This is nothing new. It has been seen throughout the Bible. Instances when the devil has tried to enslave God's people through lust and idol worship. We can especially see how quickly sin comes against you from the example of the great city of Babylon and their army's swift raid against the city of God in Jerusalem. What you open your heart up to can come back to enslave you. Don't Bow!

Don't Bow
Standing against the Idols of Our Generation

Chapter One Review

- The word image is defined as a physical likeness or representation of a person, animal, or thing; it is photographed, painted, sculptured, or otherwise made visible.

- The word Idol is defined as an image or other material object representing a deity to which religious worship is addressed. Any person or thing regarded with blind admiration, adoration, or devotion.

- The music and entertainment industries take a created image of a person or thing and lift it up as an idol for our generation to follow.

- The enemy wants to rob you and force you to become an idol worshiper but we must refuse to bow down to the idols of our generation.

Chapter One Reflection

- Take five minutes and reflect on what images are being feed to your spirit on a daily basis that will undoubtedly tear you down and put a false image of your identity and purpose within your heart.

- After you have reflected say this quick prayer: "Lord Jesus, I submit my heart to you and I ask that you rid my life of any idol that I have willingly or unwillingly worshiped. I give you all the glory and honor. Amen.

Don't Bow
Standing against the Idols of Our Generation

2

Babylon the Great

Imagine if you were going about your normal routine in the morning. The alarm clock goes off and you decide to get up and start your day. You take a quick shower and brush your teeth, comb your hair and get dressed for the day. You head out of the house and get to your destination. Suddenly a foreign military group comes into your school or place of employment and strips your freedom without notice. You are separated from your family and loved ones. Your personal belongings are confiscated. Any and everything that is important to you is gone. You find yourself locked in chains and carried off into exile to a foreign land as slaves. This is what literally happened to the Israelites as a massive Babylonian army came in and snatched up the holy city of Jerusalem.

News flash, Babylon is a typology of sin. It represents the world and its system of living. Just like the Babylonian army came and enslaved the Israelites, sin is looking to come into your life and lock you up and bring you into a system of idol worship. For some of us we have never been handcuffed before in our lives. There is a phase in the locking up process when your heart speeds up and you are thinking to yourself, "This is surreal!" Then you start to feel the pain of the handcuffs snapping and locking together putting pressure on your wrists. It becomes a physical and mental reminder that

11

you have been caught. Fear, intimidation, and helplessness are all the emotions you can experience when sin gets a hold on you. Can you think back on a time in your life that you have been caught doing something or you played things a little too close to the edge and you slipped and fell? Sin is always looking to jump on you like a lion does its prey, attacking the victim unaware with no mercy to be found.

The enemy wants to take you away from the presence of God. He desires to take your attention away from Jesus Christ and His holiness and place it on material things that will lead you astray. This enslavement and exile narrative comes from the book of Daniel which I aim to unpack over the next few chapters of this book.

In Daniel chapter one the Bible shares the story of Israel's exile into Babylon. It opens up showing the suddenness of Babylon's charge toward Jerusalem and the capturing of God's people. Sin always comes quick and unexpectedly. Please don't play with sin. Don't over rationalize what qualifies as a sin either. That is the enemy's plight to have you play close to the edge. Anything that takes you further away from God would constitute as a sin. I will be the first to tell you that sin is very strategic about its plans against our generation. The adversary is crafty in his dealings, especially when it comes to a group of promising young people.

If you were a criminal detained and placed into a police car your initial thought would be that you were primed for jail or prison. How would you feel if instead of that fate, you ended up at a facility where others were brought and released to participate in royal training? One would probably be confused yet open to the restricted freedom. This is exactly what happened to Daniel and many other Israelite youth when they came into the kingdom of Babylon. Appearances can be deceiving. Although the children of Israel were no longer free at this time, it wasn't the cruel prison experience that would be expected. Many Israelite youth were introduced to the royal courts of Babylon to be educated and used by the kingdom. This place was something entirely different than what the Israelites were accustomed to in Jerusalem. Although many of the young men had a promising future, Babylon was looking to take advantage of that promise on their lives and turn it for their own secular benefit. In the same way the world is looking to take advantage of young people's talent for their own interests. Don't allow the enemy to steal what God has given you.

Now what about this tantalizing kingdom of ancient Mesopotamia? Why is it so significant? In one simple phrase to describe it, Babylon was off the chain. Some of the greatest cities in America today are barely comparable to Babylon. Considered one of the Seven Wonders of the World, Babylon had amazing architecture in its hanging gardens and majestic defense walls. Babylon had enormous palace complexes and was home to a host of temples large and small. The Euphrates River flowed in the city and culture was prevalent. Babylon had intersections in its city streets and large three and four story high buildings. The scripture records Babylon's king exhorting the following in Daniel 4:30,

- "And the king answered and said, "Is not this great Babylon, which I have built by my mighty power as a royal residence and for the glory of my majesty?"

Idols are always looking to build themselves up. They desire to show off their majesty for their own glory. Children of God are looking to reflect the glory of Jesus to the world and none of our own. This is a main difference between the two forces. The world's greatest empire at that particular time in history was simply stunning. The lust of man was on full display. Whatever you wanted it was available. To the average eye observing Babylon and all its splendor w o u l d t h i n k, "This couldn't be too bad, after all what's wrong with getting turned up? What's wrong with a little party?

What's wrong with drinking? What's wrong with smoking? What's wrong with engaging in relationships that do not please Jesus as long as it makes me happy and nobody gets hurt? These are the questions our generation is asking.

Babylon had it all. For many of the enslaved young people that came to this city in chains, they were now willing to be chained spiritually for moments of compromise. Many of the Israelites had forsaken their relationship with the almighty God for fear of isolation and death, not understanding idol worship would bring an even greater spiritual death to their life.

Pull out a map of America and pin point the party centers of our nation. One would find large concentrations on college campuses throughout the nation as well as in the large metropolitan areas. In the Midwest we have some of the largest attended colleges and universities in the country. Unfortunately many of our youth go to these institutions of higher learning only to be faced with decisions of compromise. Instead of buffing against the majority of their peers, they decide to bow down to the most common idols in our society today.

Most Christian teenagers who leave home to attend college at a public or private institution graduate from that place of higher education and are further away from Jesus Christ, if not gone all together. Research reveals that more than two-thirds of young adults who attended a protestant church for at least a year in high school will stop attending church regularly for at least a year between the ages of 18 and 22[1].

At the college campus many alternatives have been offered to the youth of our nation. Various student organizations, clubs, fraternities, sororities, sports teams, and even the academic field have been opened up with opportunities to bow down. Jesus Christ has been pushed out of these categories all together. This is not to say that every group listed has no Christian representation, but a majority have either stiffened in their stance of evangelism within these settings or pushed a tolerance of an "all religions lead to God" agenda that downgrades the person of Jesus Christ! This is literally happening throughout the hotbeds of our country.

Miami, Los Angeles, New York City, Atlanta, Detroit, Chicago, Seattle, Cleveland, St. Louis among many others are beautiful cities but have aided in the promotion of images and idols through the secular media. New York City alone has thousands of billboards set up to catch the attention of those walking or driving throughout the city. How many of those images bring glory to Jesus? Am I saying that these cities are bad and if a person lives there they are subject to those images? No. At the same time many young people aspire to make it big in these cities but find themselves in compromising situations.

At the blink of an eye the desire for worldly pleasures will have a young person make a conscious decision to bow down to any of today's idols. Another forgotten area we are seeing an increase of youth engagement pertaining to parties, drugs, and alcohol are in the suburban areas of our cities. Often times the media focuses on the violence, sex, and drugs of inner cities but we are facing an equally alarming pandemic in the suburbs where meth labs are being built, and where marijuana and alcohol is readily available. In addition, every day in the United States, an average of 2,000 teenagers use prescription drugs without a doctor's guidance for the first time [2]. We have to wake up to what is going on around us.

Remember that I said the enemy is strategic in his plan to enslave you spiritually? Well his plan is to take out the next generation through idol worship. Those who have been called to lead the youth of this nation into the presence of God are being influenced to turn in the opposite direction and lead our generation to destruction. In the book of Daniel the king commanded his chief eunuch to bind up and bring the young people of the royal court of Israel to Babylon. Did you know that you are considered royalty? When you receive Jesus in your life you become a child of the King. Not only does the Lord know who you are but the enemy apparently does too.

This is why the enemy is looking to capture you. He never wants you to realize who you can be when Jesus is on your side and you commit to His ways. The devil is afraid of the influence you will have in the kingdom of God and in the earth as an ambassador of reconciliation. This means that God will use you to bring people to a real relationship with Jesus. The barrier that divided people from God no longer stands. You have a great call on your life and you should never forget that.

The Bible then goes on to describe in Daniel 1:4 the various attributes the eunuch identified when picking the young men for the royal court. They are as follows:

- Royalty

- Nobility

- Without blemish

- Good appearance

- Skillful in all wisdom

- Endowed with knowledge

- Understanding learning (science)

- The ability to stand in the king's palace, or a place of significance, importance, and power

- Someone who could learn the literature and language of the Chaldeans (intercultural skills)

You have been identified as someone with such great promise that you are worth going after. Unfortunately, a large percentage of teenagers do not know how valuable they are in the eyes of God. The Apostle Peter speaks to the attributes of God's children in the New Testament as well. In 1 Peter 2:9 it says:

- "But you are not like that, for you are a chosen people. You are royal priests, a holy nation, God's very own possession. As a result, you can show others the goodness of God, for he called you out of the darkness into his wonderful light" (*New Living Translation*, 2008)."

You are important. Not only does the enemy know you're royalty but he understands your capacity for greatness. You have to know that you are someone with talent, skill, and knowledge. For far too long, young people have been discouraged regarding their gifts, talents, and abilities. Maybe you did not have a father to validate you, or you never had the opportunity to express yourself through artistic endeavors or sporting events. Our youth are looking for validation from the world when they should receive encouragement from the church daily.

Even if you did not know it before, you are destined for greatness. This is why you are in the fight of your life. In Babylon these very talented young people would soon be faced with a decision. Despite their talent the goal was to have them bow down to the massive created image of the Babylonian king, and to be used for the system's secular goals. Please understand that outside of God you can never achieve your true purpose.

I know what you may be thinking, "But what if I really work hard? "What if I get all the money I need to achieve my goals?" You may also be saying, "But I know someone else who made it out of the hood or their place of poverty who is now rich and doesn't go to church." My answer comes directly from scripture. The Bible records in Matthew 5:45 the following:

- "So that you may be sons of your Father who is in heaven. For he makes his sun rise on the evil and on the good, and sends rain on the just and on the unjust."

The Lord allows for some things in life to be given to both ends of the spectrum, the just and the unjust. More than anything this shows His unending love for His creation and great display of His mercy, but by no means is it an approval of an ungodly lifestyle.

I would also say that your purpose is both simple and complex. It becomes simple when you submit to Jesus and His plan for you. It becomes complex when you don't. The enemy knows that there is a purpose and destiny for each and every young person in our generation. His goal is the same as it always has been, to steal, kill and destroy you and your God given future. Maybe you have achieved some things in your life thus far. Maybe you haven't. Maybe you are not sure of yourself and where you are going. The best way to be confident in your life's direction is to be guided by the one who gave you that life and designed the purpose for it.

What if I said that how you respond to three key challenges by the enemy could bring about a change in culture and bring glory to the Father? This is exactly what Daniel and the Hebrew boys did when they refused to bow down. You may have the same opportunity.

You may be going through these challenges at this very moment. One of the best ways to overcome an obstacle is to identify the success of others before you. Daniel overcame the many challenges he faced in his generation. The three Hebrew boys did it too. Now it's your turn to stand against the idols of our generation. Don't Bow!

Don't Bow
Standing against the Idols of Our Generation

Chapter Two Review
- Babylon is symbolic for sin and the world's system. Modern day cities, college towns, and suburban areas are similar to this historic landmark because of their lustful desires.
- The enemy desires to take you away from the presence of God and shift your mind to idol worship like the story recorded in the book of Daniel.
- The enemy knows your worth. Just like the Hebrew boys, as a child of God you are royalty and the enemy sees that as valuable to his kingdom. This is part of the reason you are attacked by our adversary in the area of idol worship.
- The devil's goal is to take out the next generation of Godly leaders but we must refuse to bow down.

Chapter Two Reflection
- Take five minutes and envision yourself as royalty walking in your place of influence (high school, college, work, etc.). You must understand that because you are a child of King Jesus, you are royalty and you have a capacity for greatness. No image or idol can make you.
- After you have reflected write down the royal characteristics described on p. 16 and say the following prayer: "Lord, I believe your word is true and that I am royalty. I agree with every characteristic listed and I declare by faith that I will exhibit them in my place of influence. I will not bow down to Babylon! Amen.

Don't Bow
Standing against the Idols of Our Generation

3

The Three Challenges

- *THE CHALLENGE OF CONSUMPTION – WHAT YOU EAT*

In the book of Daniel I identified three challenges that Babylon presented before the children of Israel while in exile. These three opportunities will determine if you will bow down or if you will stand against the idols of our generation. The first challenge is The Challenge of Consumption. The Bible records in Daniel chapter one that the king assigned them a daily portion of the food that he ate, and of the wine that he drank. Remember the definition of an Idol given earlier? It was defined as anything that is worshiped blindly with admiration, adoration, and devotion. This was not a one - time feast and worship event. This was meant to become a part of their daily routine as pupils in the king's court. The devil doesn't want any part-time lovers. He wants you to consume his food on a daily basis.

What makes this challenge interesting is that Daniel and the Hebrew boys never consumed what was being offered to them at any point in their lives while in Jerusalem. According to Jewish law, Daniel could not consume the type of food that was being provided at the king's table. Not only from a religious stand point was it inadequate for them, but physically it could harm their bodies. To add insult to injury the meat would be thrown on the floor and sacrificed to Babylonian gods. To eat anything offered up in this manor would be considered idolatry. My question to you is what are you consuming that has been sacrificed to the idols of our generation? What are you participating in that could be considered idolatry against God?

Does your consumption consist of the music being played on the local radio station and on the popular television networks? The nature of the music has progressively gotten worse in its tolerance for sex, drugs, lust and other forms of perversion. I am a young man but within the decade that I have been out of high school, the music I listened to and what is playing now is vastly different. It only takes one generation in a family that doesn't know the ways, character, and works of God for disaster to strike! The nation of Israel went through something similar. Judges 2:10 states the following:

- "After that generation died, another generation grew up who did not acknowledge the LORD or remember the mighty things he had done for Israel."

A whole generation grew up never hearing the story of God's deliverance at the Red Sea. How depressing is it that we live in a similar time. Many of our youth are growing up never knowing the sacrifice Jesus made for them at Calvary. We must be better.

Thousands of our children hear this music with no remorse or consciousness of what is entering into their hearts. We have to be honest with ourselves. If you were to play most of what we listen to in front of the elders of the prior generation we would be embarrassed for them. What if a younger sibling was in your car or in your room and the vulgar lyrics we listen to entered into their precious and innocent ears? Wake up people. We have a responsibility.

Does what you listen to and consume into your heart skew the image of relationships that God put in place at the very beginning of time? Is it shaped into something that God never intended? Our interactions in regards to relationships are primarily based upon lust and not true love. When I say true love I am speaking to the sacrificial love that Jesus displayed for His creation. The most memorized scripture amongst Christians shares this idea in John 3:16,

- "For God so loved the world, that he gave his only Son, that whoever believes in him should not perish but have eternal life."

Jesus gave knowing that some would not receive His love. Despite this, those who do accept His sacrifice receive eternal life. The opposite happens when we bow down to idols and receive their offering. We receive more emptiness.

The intellect of our generation is off the charts. We are very creative in changing the meaning of a thing into something entirely different than its true definition. By doing this we come up with terms that fit our agenda and will ultimately work for us. We have so redefined love and relationships until it meets our uncommitted appetite and has become the societal standard.

Too often we have seen celebrities give off a backwards feel for relationships. We see no signs of faithfulness but rather we see couples giving up when things get hard. We see match-making reality television shows and seem to believe that is true. This is the image portrayed in the media and we are consuming it daily. Just ask the youth in our middle and high schools how they feel about relationships. Much of their perception is determined by what they see or consume on TV and what they witness in their own homes. The vicious cycle of failed commitment does so much in the mind. It brings the pre-conceived image of fathers down to depressing levels because they are not present in the lives of our youth. Due to this behavior our generation ends up facing a much larger problem.

Hip hop has become the father of our young men. To be clear I am not referring to the art form of rap. Throughout the kingdom of God there are many individuals gifted in the ability to deliver the Gospel in this art form. I am talking about a way of life. It is not just a genre of music, but a sub-culture that has shown its face across the globe and the fatherless have been adopted by it. Idols have been lifted up in the hip hop industry to capture the imagination of our generation. Young people of all ethnic backgrounds have meshed into the sub-culture of hip hop. I've shared some of the language that is used commonly in teenage circles. It doesn't stop there but clothing trends, hair styles, piercings, tattoos are all a part of the sub-culture. This is one of the main competitors for our youth as they are faced with a large majority of peers infused into the lifestyle of hip-hop. The troubling thing is the amount of families that ignore the sounds that come from their children's rooms. We close our eyes to what's truly going on in our generation in hopes that it will go away. If no one stands up the flood gates will open up against our youth. We see this now with the increase of sexual activity among teenagers in our country.

Our generation has accepted the idea of pre-marital sex and considers it the norm. Any internet search engine could bring up the most recent statistics as it pertains to sexually transmitted diseases and pre-marital sex among our generation [3]. We no longer see commitment in any relationship nor do we seem to care much about our bodies. Hip-hop and Rock and Roll magazines glorify sex and drugs as we see it at every grocery store counter and express line in America. These are all images that are portrayed to our generation. Any smart business man will place these items in an area for easy accessibility and for impulse shoppers to consume. Our generation is becoming impulsive with idol worship and the enemy is placing his traps right in front of us. We are being desensitized to these images and because we see them so frequently the shock value is non-existent even when the image is beyond controversial. Not only have these desires become more evident and lifted into a place of prominence in the lives of our youth, but the love of money is also gripping our generation tight.

The desire for money has reached an all-time high among young people today. Due to an over emphasis of material gain and success, our generation feels less accomplished and that it has no value when they have limited resources. This is even more evident if the young person does not have certain material objects in his or her possession. If you do not have the latest and greatest in fashion, electronics, and transportation then you are considered to have no swag. It is essential to provide a working definition for this term. **Swag** is to have extreme confidence in oneself, in one's appearance, and status according to the world's standard.

Young people are bowing down to images and idols of monetary gain on a daily basis. Young men are getting involved in the selling of drugs at rapid rates. If it's not drugs it's stealing what doesn't belong to them, all for the cause of looking like you have something. Our young women are accepting gifts in the form of money, jewelry, and other benefits. In addition, our young women are becoming more "player savvy" than our young men which is saddening to say the least.

When my pastor and I first preached this message we set a demonstration of a table full of things to consume that was similar to the table that was before Daniel and the Hebrew boys in Babylon. We had raw meat and grape juice on the table. It was decorated in royal colors with fine china dishes and beautiful wine glasses. We brought several of our young people to the table to partake of this meal. As we began to entice them in this illustration to eat or consume this meat many refused, but as the stakes got higher many started to bend on their moral and spiritual stance.

The factor that moved things in our favor as makeshift kings of the Babylonian court was the offer of monetary gain. Not only our young people, but many throughout the country will do almost anything for money. We started out with $20. We asked the question, "Will you eat this raw meat for $20?" Many said no. We upped the ante to $50. Many started to get excited for an opportunity to get the money we were offering. Then we moved to $100. Youth were jumping out of their seats to get the cash we had on hand.

Now by no means would we ever allow for our youth group to eat raw meat but we had to bring the visual alive. The enemy of our souls does the exact same thing. He knows our pressure point and when to apply it. He thinks he understands when we will cave in and consume what he is offering. Unfortunately, for a large percentage of our youth that pressure point is money.

Why is this? One direct link is found in a materialistic world. Technology is so rapid in its advancement that what once took years to update can actually happen several times a year. This is seen with the latest cell phones, laptops and gaming systems. We are trying to keep up with the Idol Jones'.

Intolerance for Christianity is another limelight subject that is shown in the media, in our schools, in the work place and various other locations and secular arenas. The world doesn't want you to display your faith but it wants you to keep your mouth shut. The world wants you to have a tolerance to all religions despite your Christian convictions. This does not mean that you do not love all people with the love of Jesus, but rather you remain committed to the Bible and how it directs you to conduct your life as a Christian. This is just another area of consumption that keeps you bound and unable to bring others into the kingdom of God.

Never have drugs and alcohol been as fashionable as they are now. From the music that plays daily, to the movies we watch at the theater, drugs and alcohol are before our faces. As I am writing this book the newest craze in illegal drugs is known as "Molly"[4]. This drug is rapped about by several artists and is portrayed as a high compared to no other. A deadly mixture of drugs, "Molly" is affecting the lives of our young people in large numbers. The reason our generation is addicted to all types of drugs is because they are looking for a release from life. Experimentation is happening almost every weekend among the youth of our cities. Consumption in this area goes hand in hand with the party lifestyle. Young people are looking to enjoy the lusts of life without any idea of the consequences that come with participating in these environments. It's more than doing the latest dance moves and trying the latest alcoholic beverage or drug. The lives of young people are being taken! Drunk driving, overdosing on drugs, and sexual activity are results of the careless lifestyle many of us are living. Unfortunately, we only see certain sides of the story when watching these environments on many of the current reality TV shows. The enemy has glorified drunkenness, getting high and sleeping with people. This is not true fulfillment.

Another area that is shown to us consistently is the image of failed minority groups. Many African-Americans, Latinos, and other minorities are portrayed as failures. While there is some truth to the failure of our school systems and their ability to help educate a generation of under privileged students, minorities are not failures. Someone needs to know that you are not a failure because of the color of your skin. Not all young people from rough neighborhoods are destined to fail in society. Our nation needs more mentors to pour into the next generation a message of hope that when Jesus is in your life all things are possible, even becoming successful when the odds are against you! We need more examples in the business world, in medicine, in education, in sports, and yes even in entertainment. We need Christ like individuals leading the charge of shaping the next generation.

These are the elements of the first challenge of Babylon. To have you consume unhealthy images that can destroy your vision, your confidence, and have you chasing after a false reality. Again I ask the question, what are you eating? What are you consuming that is bringing destruction to your life? Will you cave in to the world's lustful appetite or prove like Daniel that God's diet is better?

- ## *THE CHALLENGE OF IDENTITY – WHO YOU ARE*

Not only does the world want you to consume the various strongholds it delivers, but it also wants to change your identity. The Bible says in Daniel chapter one that the eunuch changed the names of the Hebrew boys. When the enemy changes your name he is looking to show his power over you and change who God made you to be.

Daniel whose name in Hebrew means "God is my judge" became known as Belteshazzar which means "lord of the straitened treasure, prince who Bel favours." Hananiah whose name means "God has favored" became known as Shadrach "the great scribe, little friend of the king." Mishael's name means "who is what God is" became known as Meshach which means "guest of a king", and his name is also thought to be that of a Chaldean god. Azariah which means "Jehovah has helped" became known as Abed-nego which means "servant of Nebo, worshipper of Mercury." Ok, so what does all this mean? The bottom line is this. That God created you and named you. The Bible declares in Jeremiah 1:5 the following:

- "Before I formed you in the womb I knew you, and before you were born I consecrated you; I appointed you a prophet to the nations."

28

God has shaped you in His image and has given you a specific identity. That very identity is rooted in Jesus Christ. The enemy's job is to distort that image and change that identity to further his plan and agenda. He aims to destroy an entire generation through idol worship and a false sense of self. He wants you to embrace a false identity.

What has the enemy labeled you with? Has he called you ugly? Has he labeled you as a nobody? Has he called you poor and unsuccessful? Has he labeled you promiscuous and a drug addict? What about an alcoholic or any other label that God did not place upon you? Satan is the father of lies and is not to be believed.

Everything that the devil does is backwards and counterfeit. God was the first to change someone's name. Not to tear them down but to lift them up. When God gave new names to his people it further established who they were as a child of God and had clues to their destiny within the name. Here are a few examples:

- **Abram** whose name meant exalted father became **Abraham** which means father of a multitude.

  o Gen. 17:5 says, "No longer shall your name be called Abram, but your name shall be Abraham, for I have made you the father of a multitude of nations.

- **Jacob** whose name means heel holder, supplanter, trickster became known as **Israel** which means God prevails.

29

o Gen. 35:10 says, "And God said to him, "Your name is Jacob; no longer shall your name be called Jacob, but Israel shall be your name." So he called his name Israel."

- **Saul** whose name means desired became **Paul** whose name means small or little. He was no longer the desired one to persecute the Jews but became small and humbled so that God's glory could be revealed and salvation could come to the gentiles.

o Acts 13:9 says, "Saul, also known as Paul, was filled with the Holy Spirit, and he looked the sorcerer in the eye." (New Living Translation, 2008).

These are just a few examples of positive name changes. In 2 Cor. 5:17 the Apostle Paul says this:

- "Therefore, if anyone is in Christ, he is a new creation. The old has passed away; behold, the new has come."

In Christ you are a totally new person. The old things that you may have done, the things that you are ashamed to tell anyone about, the old habits and problems no longer hold you.

In Christ you have a new identity as a son or daughter of the King! Your identity is secure in the one that gave it to you. His name is Jesus. You do not have to bow down to images of secular artists. Don't desire to be like them because their identity is not real. It's made up for mass appeal. In no other place is this maybe more evident than in the modeling industry.

In any of the modeling reality television shows many of the models are beautiful just the way they are but many have had things done to them to further their appearance and change their identity. Please hear my cry, do not be influenced by the world and allow them to change who you are in Jesus. This is not to say there won't be challenges you face when trying to hold on to what the Lord has given you, but at least you will be authentic and not plastic.

Even though the eunuch changed the names of Daniel and the Hebrew boys they never embodied the change. They knew that they were children of God that lived by a certain standard and would not allow any label to change who they were.

- ### *THE CHALLENGE OF WORSHIP – GOD VS. IDOLS*

The third challenge is a huge one. As previously shared, God has always been jealous when his bride worships someone other than Him. What person wouldn't be offended if the love of their life participated in an affair? The Bible records this challenge in Daniel chapter three. In verse one it states:

- "King Nebuchadnezzar made a gold statue ninety feet tall and nine feet wide and set it up on the plain of Dura in the province of Babylon (*New Living Translation*, 2008)."

This idol was to be different from all of the others in Babylon. Even though there were small idols and false gods throughout the land, this particular idol would be a public display of

31

worship. The huge golden statue was placed in the plain of Dura which would have been an area where thousands could gather and all worship together. This would have been a highly visible area. The enemy's goal is for you to make a public confession of who you worship.

Consumption can be hidden. You can eat certain foods when nobody is around. Embarrassed about your appetite? Wait until the midnight hour to feed your flesh. Want to be someone else with a different look and identity? Hide your true image and mask yourself with secularism. These are the tricks of the enemy. Rather, these are the set-ups of the enemy all leading to the third challenge. In this one, you can't sit on the side lines. You cannot be a bench warmer. You have to get in the game. His ultimate goal is for you to pledge allegiance to his kingdom and be a full fledge idol worshiper. The Bible says that all the public officials came to the dedication of this idol. This included – every people group, every nation, and every language. It doesn't matter who you are, where you are from, or what you look like the enemy will challenge you to find out who you worship.

Further in the text of Daniel, the herald proclaimed that when the people heard the sound of the horn, pipe, lyre, trigon, harp, bagpipe, and every kind of music, they were to fall down and worship the golden image that King Nebuchadnezzar had set up. I suggest to you that it's not a coincidence that music is the call for you to bow down.

When I was high school I loved to dance. In the Metro Detroit area we would listen to a certain type of music that when it came on you knew it was time to hit the floor and dance. The guys would stand along the wall; fashionable in the latest fitted baseball cap, designer jeans and a nice pair of Nike Air Force one gym shoes. We would watch the party with anticipation of the **SOUND**. All of a sudden, **GODZILLA,** the greatest dance track of my teenage years would play!

This particular song had a rhythmic beat out of this world. It was everyone's favorite and the calling card for the next level of engagement or in today's term, time to "Turn Up". At the sound of Godzilla all the girls would rush the floor and the boys would slap high fives and get out there too. The question I have is what is the sound that engages you? What voice at the midnight hour calls to you to engage in fornication? What call or text or tweet comes across your cell phone to go out and drink and smoke? What image comes across the screen of your life that makes you bow down? Just like the days of Daniel our generation is triggered to bow down through the music that we listen to.

Isn't it interesting that Lucifer was known for his worship and musical ability, but ultimately it was his rebellion that got him kicked out of heaven? Does what you're listening to rehearse in your spirit, it's all about me? Is what your listening to sow seeds of rebellion? Is what your listening to making a mockery of God's true intention for relationships and marriage? Does what you're watching embody an unhealthy image of sexuality?

These are the questions that I pose to our generation. Daniel 3:6 states the consequences to disobeying the decree to bow down to the idol image. It says:

- "And whoever does not fall down and worship shall immediately be cast into a burning fiery furnace."

Are you willing to face the heat to keep your integrity? Are you willing to stand in the fire to keep your identity?

Now here comes the interesting part. In Daniel 3:8-12 the Bible says that as soon as this decree went out a certain group of Chaldeans came forward and maliciously accused the Jews. I would like to highlight two more working definitions for the words malicious and accused as follows:

- **Malicious** comes from the root word malice which means - desire to inflict injury, harm, or suffering on another, either because of a hostile impulse or out of deep-seated meanness.

- **Accused** means to be charged with a crime, wrongdoing, or fault.

The point of the definition is this, whenever you make a conscious decision that you want to live for God, your enemies also known as your haters, will come out against you. They want to bring malicious accusations against you. They want to inflict spiritual injury, harm and suffering to you through their deep-rooted meanness. This is accomplished by false accusations of a particular crime you committed.

Where are malicious accusations prevalent today? It is in thousands of high schools across our country. Peer pressure is the pre-cursor. If you show any glimpse of faithfulness to Jesus along with conservative morals and values you are a prime target for testing. Does this happen everywhere? No. Does it happen often enough to have an impact on our generation? Without a doubt. In the eyes of our society and in the case of youth popularity, you have genuinely committed a crime when you stand up for what you believe in, especially something as controversial as Christianity. As long as you do not impose your beliefs on others then you can decide to believe and practice whatever you want. Is this the way Jesus intended for us to live, by not sharing our faith? Jesus commanded us to do the exact opposite by going out and making disciples.

Daniel at the time of this intense trial had been raised up into a prominent position in the kingdom. Even though the Hebrew boys' names had been changed they didn't embody that new identity. They refused to eat the meat of idols, thus holding on to the things of God. No matter what someone says about you don't allow their words to deter you from following

Jesus. Unfortunately, sometimes even your peers are dead set on conspiring against you.

The Chaldeans told the king in Daniel chapter three that Shadrach, Meshach, and Abednego do not serve the gods of Babylon and that they will not bow to the golden image. These are the type of people around you that will test your commitment to Jesus. They want to see what you will do in an environment filled with secular music and television. In a world where sex is glorified and purity is frowned upon. Your enemy wants to see what you will do when you are alone with someone of the opposite sex and the parents are not due to be back in the house until the next day. They long to see what you will do when you go through a period of disappointment when someone close to you has let you down. How will you respond?

When you continue on in chapter three of the book of Daniel you get the response of the king to the Hebrew boys who boldly refused to bow down to the golden image. He becomes furious. You must understand what it does to the enemy when you stand on righteousness and with passion decide to serve Jesus. So my question is what will you do when you're faced with a decision of who you will worship? Worship is not something you only do while listening to music, but worship is a lifestyle. It is exemplified in the choices that you make on a daily basis. It is how you treat and love other people. It is how you reverence Jesus and how you commit to His ways.

The Hebrew boys made a conscious decision that they would not compromise their relationship with God. Daniel 3:17-18 should be your response to opposition from the enemy and his challenge of Idol worship. It states:

- "If this be so, our God whom we serve is able to deliver us from the burning fiery furnace, and he will deliver us out of your hand, O king. But if not, be it known to you, O king, that we will not serve your gods or worship the golden image that you have set up."

What great courage to stand in the face of a powerful man who is able to destroy you, who can humiliate you, and send you to a burning fire. These are the type of radical youth Jesus is looking for today. When an entire generation decides to bow down to the images and idols of our society, someone has to stand up and refuse to be like everyone else. If you decide to be tossed into the fire you may just find something you never expected. Don't Bow!

Don't Bow
Standing against the Idols of our Generation

Chapter Three Review
- The book of Daniel highlights three challenges from the enemy that are placed before God's people.
- **The Challenge of Consumption** – what you eat. Just like the Hebrew boys were presented with foreign food that was not healthy for them spiritually or physically our enemy places things in front of us that become deadly consumption.
- **The Challenge of Identity** – who you are. Just as the Hebrew boy's names were changed, the enemy looks to change your identity by labeling you with titles that are not God ordained.
- **The Challenge of Worship** – God vs. Idols. The enemy wants to see who your allegiance is to through worship. In this time you cannot hide in regards to who you worship. Society will bring out your confession.
- If you refuse to bow down to these challenges God's Glory will be revealed in your life.

Chapter Three Reflection
- Have you experienced the three challenges? If so, have you passed or failed? Either way recite the following prayer: "Lord, help me to bring glory to your name when faced with the challenges. Give me boldness like the Hebrew boys to refuse to bow down to any image or idol. In Jesus name, Amen."

4

In the Fire

In the state of Michigan the months of July and August are usually the hottest. Temperatures are consistently in the upper 80's. Further south I can imagine the average day being a lot hotter than that. Regions in the tropics certainly would be thought of as extreme compared to our conditions. Even on the hottest day in my city I could not imagine what it felt like to be surrounded by fire like the Hebrew boys.

Daniel chapter three continues to tell the story of their defiance to the Babylonian king and his mandate to worship the golden image. Out of fury, he commanded that the furnace be turned up seven times hotter than it was usually heated. Your enemy understands when his pride has been hurt. He knows when he is down in the game and has to deploy a full court press against you. Not only does he want to beat you but he wants to destroy you. He wants your suffering to be beyond bearable. How many of us would have fainted at the sound of the furnace intensifying in its heat?

He then ordered some of the mightiest men of his army to bind Shadrach, Meshach, and Abednego and to cast them into the burning fiery furnace. The heat had increased so quickly that when they opened the furnace the men who threw the Hebrew boys into the fire were actually burned and consumed.

News Flash! When you stand for Christ and you don't bow to images and idols, those who handled you falsely will get burned. I am not referring to a physical scorching or death but something showing that God doesn't play with those who harm his children. Every word or accusation spoken against you, every lie that materialized will be burned.

Those three men fell into the furnace bound up for making a righteous stand for God. In our day how many people can you identify with that resemble the courage the Hebrew boys exemplified? Not too many. Yet this is what Jesus is calling for. A generation of radical young men and women who are willing to stand in the face of any man and proclaim that the only God we will worship is Jesus Christ. Daniel 3:24-25 is breathtaking to read. It says the following:

- But suddenly, Nebuchadnezzar jumped up in amazement and exclaimed to his advisers, "Didn't we tie up three men and throw them into the furnace?" "Yes, Your Majesty, we certainly did," they replied. "Look!" Nebuchadnezzar shouted. "I see four men, unbound, walking around in the fire unharmed! And the fourth looks like a god!" (*New Living Translation*, 2008)

I noticed a couple things from this portion of scripture. The first thing was that the king had not taken his eyes away from the Hebrew boys while in the fire. Your enemy wants to see your demise. He is paying attention to you in the middle of the fire. Why is this? Remember his goal is to see you bow down. He wants to see if you will finally concede to his decree once the heat is turned up in your life. Will you finally bow down to the idols in your life when things get hot? Will that moment occur in the middle of a date with your girlfriend or boyfriend and you are pressured to "make out?" Will that moment occur at the party when you are among the mass majority of your peers who have all decided that compromising your morals is a part of the teenage or college life? Will you bow down in moments of depression, oppression, or sadness? What fire are you in?

The Bible says that the king was astonished. He needed a second opinion so he asked his counselors if they did indeed throw three men in the furnace. They responded with a yes. He then stated while in shock that he saw four men in the furnace first unbound. It is interesting that once the Hebrew boys where in the fire, what was holding them had to let go. In addition they were unharmed and lastly the king identified the fourth person in the fire as looking like the son of God.

Understand this youth of this generation. If you stand for righteousness and refuse to bow down to the golden images of our society, if you are thrown into the fire, God will be there with you. Thousands of young people go to bed crying on their pillow because of the fire they are in. They cannot come to grips as to why their life is so messed up. They look for validation in their parents but only seem to get ridiculed. They search for acceptance amongst their peers but continually get the cold shoulder. Yet if you reach out to Jesus things can change.

It is in the fire that God gives us revelation of His sacrifice. He shows us who He really is and who we really are. In times of great distress and pain God will show up and be a comfort to you. The Hebrew boys came out of the fire without a single piece of hair on their heads getting burned. The Lord had protected them and they were now even more on fire spiritually for God. Through this adversity the Hebrew boys were able to bring glory to the Father. If and when you stand just like the Hebrew boys, you will bring about an awareness of Jesus that was absent in the culture. You can literally bring about a shift.

These types of challenges will push you into a new level of boldness. God will show you how strong you really are. You are strong in Christ Jesus. Paul said it best in 2 Cor. 12:10,

- "For the sake of Christ, then, I am content with weaknesses, insults, hardships, persecutions, and calamities. For when I am weak, then I am strong."

You can get stronger in Jesus when faced with adversity. Unfortunately, I didn't always see this. I can remember being a young teenager trying to fit into the crowd. I was challenged in the fire to stand on righteousness but I failed to allow God to aid me. My history of growing up in church, singing in the church choir, having an amazing experience with the Holy Spirit was hidden from my friends. Of course they knew I was a Christian, whatever that meant, but I had done a great job of masking myself into who I wanted people to think I was. Just like thousands of young people today I made several decisions to bow down to the images and idols of our generation.

Conversations that occurred in the classrooms made me feel uncomfortable even if I never showed it. I decided I would participate in those talks so I would not be labeled in a way that nobody ever wants to be, a loser. I did just about everything that others were doing in my circle. I was in the fire. Instead of seeing Jesus in the midst of my adversity I turned to whatever I thought would fill the voids of my life. In the next chapter I will share with you the void that every human being has in their life and who can fill that void. Don't Bow!

Don't Bow
Standing against the Idols of Our Generation

Chapter Four Review

- When you stand for Christ and you don't bow to images and idols, those who handled you falsely will get burned.

- Your enemy wants to see if you will finally concede to his decree to bow down once the heat is turned up in your life.

- If you stand for righteousness and refuse to bow down to the golden images of our society, if you are thrown into the fire, God will be there with you.

Chapter Four Reflection

- What fires are you facing? Just like in the story of the Hebrew boys, if you display great faith and stand against the idols of our generation God will be there to comfort you. His glory will be revealed through your life.

- After reflecting on the fire I encourage you to say this prayer: "Lord, I pray that you show up for me just as you did for the Hebrew boys. It was in the middle of the fire that you showed up and comforted them. I pray that you do the same thing for me. In Jesus name, Amen."

Don't Bow
Standing against the Idols of Our Generation

5

The Heart Void

God is a master creator. There is no one else who can compare to His expertise in this field. The book of Genesis records His exploits. God was able to separate the waters, He was able to form the land and shift the heavens into place. Stars and galaxies were painted with His hands. God was able to bring life to the world. Creatures of the land, of the air, and of the sea were all brought into existence. Lastly, He was able to uniquely create mankind.

The Bible records this magnificent feat, in Gen. 2:7 it states:

- "Then the LORD God formed the man of dust from the ground and breathed into his nostrils the breath of life, and the man became a living creature."

Can you imagine God scooping up dust from an old dirt road in your hometown, then shaping that dust with precision into the form of a man? God would then blow into that newly assembled dust sculpture. At the very onset of that eternal wind entering into the dust formed nostrils and then flowing into the dust formed lungs, a once empty vessel now has become a living soul. Man was now fully functioning with

43

hands, feet, eyes, lips, and every other feature that makes us so unique. This ladies and gentlemen is our God!

The Bible also states that we, mankind were shaped in His (God's) image and likeness and that we would have dominion over the rest of the creation. He placed Adam, the one in which he created, the firstborn of all mankind in the Garden of Eden with a purpose and destiny. This is a good point to let each and every reader know that God has created you with a specific purpose. There are no mistakes with God. Yes, many of us may have grown up in tough situations but God has a plan for you.

Unfortunately, Adam and his wife Eve did not adhere to the plan, purpose, and direction of God. They were tricked by Satan into believing that they would receive understanding of how to be like God if they ate of the tree of the knowledge of good and evil. What the enemy doesn't want you to know or remember is that God has already made you like himself. You have the ability to flow in the love of God, have dominion, and be creative with the uniqueness that God has created you with. When you operate as a child of God it brings glory to the Father. The moment they ate that forbidden fruit a separation occurred in the relationship with God and mankind. A barrier was placed, denying us full access to God because of sin. This is what caused the original space for God in the heart of man, into what is called the heart void.

When God shaped mankind He placed inside each and every person a desire to be near him. Deep within the heart of every individual there is a space carved out for God to reign. God was present in this space before Adam and Eve fell. He walked with Adam, He meet with him every day and communicated his love toward him. God gave him a sense of purpose as he named the animals and worked in the garden. Sin has since created a deeper void in our hearts where God was designed to be, and the enemy has tried to jam that space with as many idols as possible.

How many people have asked the question who am I? Why am I here? What is my purpose? People ask these questions because they feel that something is missing. They feel an emptiness that cannot be explained by our objective reasoning. It is a spiritual question that requires a spiritual answer produced from an eternal source. The enemy's job is to cloud your mind and heart from ever reaching the one who has the answer. His name is Jesus.

The heart void has placed young people in very compromising situations. How many talk shows have we watched were young women and even young men have given their hearts over to a half-time lover thinking that individual would fill their heart void? They say to themselves, "If Johnny would just notice me I would be alright," or "If I had better clothing and shoes then I would be accepted". "Maybe if I gave him more things he would love me." This wishful thinking almost never happens the way we hope it will. Maybe you have had your own experience with trying to fill your heart void. The devil has always desired to take the place of God in our lives. He, from day one, has desired to be worshiped as a god. What better way to make our generation bow down to him or other false gods and idols than to try and hijack our heart space?

The image I see for this heart void is the devil taking the hinges off of the door to your heart. The door that was once placed in front of your heart void has now been replaced with a revolving door. You know the kind that are at big fortune 500 companies in your downtown area or the kinds that are installed at your local banking establishment. What is the purpose of a revolving door? To provide relatively easy access and free flowing traffic in and out of a particular edifice or building. The revolving door is to make one's visit convenient. The enemy has desired to make your heart space easily accessible and free flowing to the idols of our generation.

When one boyfriend or girlfriend is done using you then in comes another one, and another one, and you get the picture. Perhaps your struggle is not in relationships but in drugs. Many have tried this avenue as a means to fill the emptiness of their lives. They move from less impactful drugs to heavy hitters because nothing has changed with the void that they feel. Stories of young people abusing themselves through cutting are becoming more prominent. The pain felt through this act supposedly helps free them from the pain of emptiness and deprived self-worth. All of these examples are ineffective place holders for the real object.

The heart void is not always filled with negative things either. Well, let me rephrase. Not all idols appear to be as negative as others; in all actuality they are just as dangerous. Our jobs have become idol gods in our life. Many young people in our generation are seeking to be as successful as possible. So they obtain the degree, get the job offer and find themselves working tirelessly in a rat race to a never ending finish. The need to feel accomplished is a driving force of the heart void, but when an individual achieves a particular status some questions are still not answered. Again, the questions and answers are of the spiritual variety. Does my job title define me or is there something more? The enemy plays on your heart void in hopes that you will acquire a personal idol to fill it. Another tactic he uses in conjunction with the heart void is lies about your past.

Many individuals who are searching to fill their heart void are tricked into believing the reason there is a void in their heart, is due to something they did. While this is partially true due to the sin of our ancestor Adam and the affect it had on all creation, you should not feel responsible for the failed relationships and expectations by those that were not in your life. The enemy feeds you a lie that one reason you feel empty is because your father or mother was never in your life.

Maybe you are like me and you had two parents but they were separated. I had one parent whom I was living with and another parent on the other side of town. One particular moment I can remember vividly when the enemy played on my heart void. I preface this story to say that my relationship with my dad is great. I can call him now and talk about anything. Our relationship has strengthened through our interaction and the love of Jesus Christ. I pray that others will be able to be healed from this story.

During my early childhood I lived with my mother and visited my father often. He was a good dad considering the many fathers in society who have never seen their children or supported them. He did provide financially for my sister and I but one particular moment in my life left a lasting pain for many years emotionally. It was my birthday and I was turning maybe eight or nine years old. My father was set to pick me up for a day of fun festivities. As any child would do, I got up as early as possible and got dressed. I was so excited I could barely take it. So I decided to wait on my front porch for my father to pull up in the drive way and pick me up.

I waited with my little baseball cap on and back-pack strapped in case I would be staying the night. Well, minutes went by. Then hours dragged along. Before I knew it the sun was setting. Finally, my father picked me up with little time to go on the adventure I had envisioned. Instead we went to a local restaurant in which nothing on the menu an eight year old would like was presented. After dinner was finished I was dropped back off at the house with a simple gift that also didn't satisfy a young child's expectation.

I was heartbroken. I cried in my pillow that night. The enemy tried to lie to me and say I could never trust or believe in any father again, but the devil was a liar. He was trying to destroy my image of God the Father. The enemy may have also tried to distort your image of God by the interactions you had with your own father or mother. Sometimes you just don't have all the information. I never took into account what could have happened earlier in the day or if he was told certain information of a restaurant and particular present I would enjoy. Overall, what the devil meant for bad God turned it into my good. I am here to say that our Heavenly Father is good and His mercy endures forever! He is loving and faithful, so if you had a bad experience in the natural realm know that God will exceed your expectation.

Indeed there may have been some moments missed due to an absent or even tardy parent in your life, but that will not answer all of your life's questions or fill in the space specifically carved out for Jesus Christ. I learned a valuable lesson years later from that experience. That people are human and are bound to let you down from time to time but Jesus will always be there. Don't allow the enemy to take your disappointment and clear a space for idol worship.

If you sincerely seek after God and ask Him to show you your heart void He will. If you ask Him to remove the idols that seem to have taken up permanent space in your heart He will. Jesus would like nothing better than to abide in the place He has always wanted to be in which is in your heart. Maybe you are thinking it is not that simple. That what you are literally dealing with is more like a virus that you just can't get rid of. Well in the next chapter I will talk to you about the idol virus that God is ready to cure in your life. Don't bow!

Don't Bow
Standing against the Idols of Our Generation

Chapter Five Review

- God created us and shaped us in his image. He created a space in every man's heart for him.

- Due to sin that heart space has become a heart void. The enemy is looking to fill this space with every idol imaginable.

- In ignorance we try to fill our heart void with all types of things. The devil plays on this based upon past hurts.

- When we yield to the love of Jesus he will fill our heart space and bring fulfillment to our lives.

Chapter Five Reflection

- What have you tried to fill your heart void with? Jesus is the only thing that can fill that void in your life. Open up to him today and let him fill you.

- Have you experienced a failed expectation? Is there a situation the devil has tried to play on your heart void? If so, say the following prayer: "Dear Lord, I come to you in order to relinquish my grip on a past hurt. I acknowledge that the enemy has played my heart void. I also acknowledge that my heart void is designed for you to fill. So I ask now, please reign in my heart forever. In Jesus name, Amen."

Don't Bow
Standing against the Idols of Our Generation

6

The Idol Virus

In today's age it seems like everyone has a computer. It could be a laptop or a PC unit. Maybe you have something a bit sleeker like a netbook or you have decided to go with a tablet for portability. Regardless of the type of technology you possess the one thing we all dread happening to that expensive piece of equipment is suffering severe damage beyond repair. Thousands of people have been impacted in this way by the computer virus.

My freshman year of college I had a PC unit that may have been a bit out of date so I decided to get a brand new laptop. This machine had all the bells and whistles. It was of great value especially since it was brand new. As time went on I became careless with the laptop and did not renew it consistently with updates and anti-virus protection. While surfing the net one day I clicked on something that would be identified later as a computer virus. This was the beginning of my troubles.

To bring a greater understanding of this concept I want to review a few working definitions. First there is a **computer virus** which is defined as a program that enters a computer usually without the knowledge of the operator. Some viruses are mild and only cause messages to appear on the screen, but others are destructive and wipe out the computer's memory or cause more severe damage. Your heart and mind is like a computer. Just like the virus enters into the computer without the operator's knowledge we too can be infiltrated in the same way.

When I minister to young people within my youth group, they sometimes say that they don't listen to the words of rap songs but they do listen to the beat. What they do not understand is that the more you listen to something it becomes repetitive and sub-consciously enters into your spirit. Willingly or not it is infecting you. How much worse is it when we are actively participating in detrimental behavior? When you watch certain images and idols on television or on the internet you are literally allowing a virus to infect you.

As the definition described, some viruses only show up on the screen. When people look at the screen of your life what does it read? Does your screen show the image of a celebrity idol and your commitment to look and act like them? Is it seen in the way that you dress? Does your social media account represent an image that does not bring glory to the Father? What are you re-tweeting that makes your screen look corrupted? Does the message you portray give the appearance to others that you no longer view purity as sacred? Does your social media timeline show images of partying and consumption of alcohol and drugs, etc.? Your screen does matter. Due to the era we live in and the access of information, employers and college admissions departments are viewing social media now more than ever. Will your screen impact your future in a positive or negative light?

I challenge you right now to stop reading. Yes, stop reading this book right now and grab your cell phone, mobile device, or tablet and for the next five minutes search for any idol viruses that may be plaguing your screen. I am not only referring to the home screen of your cell phone but I am talking about the screen of your life! How many idol images could you find? If there are any viruses stored on your

51

electronic devices do something you should have done a long time ago and delete it! Take away the pictures that may have you in bondage. Erase the text messages that have engaged you in lustful and unfruitful conversations. Remove the phone numbers of individuals that do not have your best interest in mind. In fact clear out secondary contact information so there is no excuse to contact those people ever again. Some of you may have to go as far as changing your cell phone number. God is calling for a cleansing of your spiritual computer. Millions of youth and adults have been addicted to images of pornography. This industry has bound up men and women for decades. Research has shown that pornography is one of the most profitable businesses in the world. Sadly, one of the peak times in which pornography is sought after is on Sunday, the day we are supposed to worship our Lord. Saved and unsaved people have been tortured in their spirits by this perverse industry. It's time to stand against this idol.

These are just a few of the messages that appear on the screens of people's lives due to the idol virus but what about the more long term effects? Does what you consume delete your knowledge of God? Have you gotten so far into the world and its images and idols that you no longer acknowledge Jesus Christ and His love for you? The laptop I had purchased previously with so much joy now had gone totally black and the screen indicated that I must restart the computer. The only sign of life was a blinking cursor flashing repeatedly in the corner. The times that I neglected to properly shut down my laptop and update its software had now come back to bite me. What have you failed to properly shut down in your life?

Let this be a warning to you that a daily update of God's word and worship is essential to keeping a healthy life. When we fail to update the software of our lives our system can be bogged down with unnecessary clutter.

The Bible says in Psalm 68:19 -

- "Blessed be the Lord, who daily bears us up; God is our salvation. Selah"

Jesus desires to bear you up and give you the benefits that you need each and every day but you must receive it. Maybe you are living with an outdated hard drive that has been blown up by to many viruses over the years. Jesus is able to provide a new life for you and heal your brokenness caused by idols. The Apostle Paul says this in Romans 12:2 -

- "Don't copy the behavior and customs of this world, but let God transform you into a new person by changing the way you think. Then you will learn to know God's will for you, which is good and pleasing and perfect." (*New Living Translation*, 2008)

Don't allow an idol virus to conform you into an image that the world would be comfortable with. Allow the Holy Spirit to transform you and renew your mind so that you are empowered to stand against the idols of our generation.

It is the Lord's desire that you live for Him faithfully. He loved us so much that he died for us. There is a universal call that God is making to all of mankind. It is a call to a real relationship with him. Maybe you are saying I am just tired of dealing with the idols in my life and you're ready for a commitment. You just might be sensing the Holy Spirit calling you to something greater. In the next chapter we will highlight what that something is. Don't Bow!

Don't Bow
Standing against the Idols of Our Generation

Chapter Six Review
- The idol virus is like a computer virus that comes into your system unaware. It can cause unwanted messages to come across your screen or bring more fatal damage.
- We allow viruses to come into our heart when we do not update daily with the word of God and worship Jesus.
- Don't allow an idol virus to conform you into an image that the world would be comfortable with. Allow the Holy Spirit to transform you and renew your mind so that you are empowered to stand against the idols of our generation.

Chapter Six Reflection
- What images have infiltrated your heart and mind? If you didn't complete before, delete all of your images and messages on social media that plague your mind daily. Commit to be transformed and renewed today!
- Now that you have dealt with the idol virus say the following prayer: "Lord, I thank you for renewing my mind and empowering me to deal with the idol virus. I endeavor to seek you daily through your word and worship. In Jesus name, Amen."

Don't Bow
Standing against the Idols of Our Generation

7

The Call

God has an interesting way of totally changing your life in a blink of an eye. After high school I had decided to go to a small private college in Northwest Indiana. At that institution I would play football and study business. This had been my dream for many years to play at the collegiate level. I left my hometown ready to take on the world. Well when I got there nothing was as I planned it to be. Playing football at the college level was vastly more difficult than I anticipated. I went through a season of ongoing injuries that kept me from seeing the field. I had gone through a difficult break up with my high school sweet heart that sent me into a mini depression and on top of that I was homesick. What an experience.

I first responded to what I knew growing up. I prayed a little bit and read the Bible until it got boring to me. Once again I just wanted to fit in and be accepted by my peers so I began to participate in the so called extra-curricular activities. Again not wanting to go against the grain I went to the parties just like most college kids did. I remember one particular party that impacted me greatly. My roommates and buddies where headed to a fraternity house that was hosting a glow stick party. My curiosity was at an all-time high considering my spirit was so low and I was looking for anything to make me feel better.

55

This is a conventional tactic of the devil, to introduce an idol to you in your moment of weakness.

We all put on white T-shirts so the black lighting could catch the glowing highlights and words we drew on them. We had glow sticks in our hands and around our necks. I literally said to myself that I hurt so badly and that God hadn't been there for me that I was ready to live a life outside of him and enjoy it. I am positive that there are thousands of young people that feel the exact same way. I am here to tell you that despite these feelings God truly cares for you and will blow your mind with his ultimate plan for your life.

I walked into the basement were people where dancing, smoking, and drinking ready to live my life. I remember walking looking around the basement for a safe place to both engage in the party yet I could be reserved from stepping all the way out too quickly. The weirdest thing happened in the mist of the loud music and drinking. I heard the voice of God. Just four simple words, "Why are you here?" Immediately convicted and feeling sick to my stomach I told my roommate that I would be leaving for the night and I returned to my dorm room. I cried out to God because in the midst of my pain and confusion he rescued me with a rhetorical question.

I want to ask every reader the same question that God asked me, "Why are you here?" I do not know what your "here" is but, it could be that you are in the middle of adulterous situation. Not from a married perspective but in regards to your relationship with Jesus. You could be as far away from God as imaginable. Maybe you feel the same way I did, that the reason you did interact with the idols of our generation is because of the hurt and pain you were going through. The good thing is you have an example. You don't have to be depressed and broken and give yourself to idolatry based upon a feeling. Jesus has the ability to set you free.

It reminds me of one of the more familiar passages of scripture in the Bible. In John chapter four we see the story of the Samaritan women who had gone through a tough patch in her life. The Bible says that she had gone through a series of husbands and the man she was currently with was not hers. Who knows what this woman had gone through? More than likely she experienced disappointment, failure, and pain. She probably felt disconnected to others in society, especially the other women based upon the time in which she went to draw water from the well. The woman probably wanted to avoid others who may have looked down on her due to her current situation.

You could guess that she felt safe in the isolation. Many young people today have isolated themselves due to the pain they feel. Not having anyone to befriend them, encourage them, stick up for them or let them know they are loved and appreciated. The enemy loves this situation because he will find someone or something to place in your life as a distraction. Please know that Jesus sees your situation and he will come to you just as he did this Samaritan woman.

The Bible says that Jesus told the disciples that He had to go through Samaria. This was indeed taking Him off the path of His original destination but He felt the cry of this women's heart. She was knee deep in adultery and He had to save her. He gets to the well and He begins to engage her in conversation. He asks her for a drink. Noticing that He was a Jew she responds out of her religious and cultural experience knowing that Jews and Samaritans do not interact. He then responds back to her by saying in John 4:10 -

- "Jesus answered her, "If you knew the gift of God, and who it is that is saying to you, 'Give me a drink,' you would have asked him, and he would have given you living water.""

The issue again for many is that we are thirsty for something real. We have been played time and time again by the enemy who does not have the ability to bring true fulfillment. Our generation has been drinking from the wells of idols long enough. Jesus is the one who can provide living water that will fill us spiritually.

Jesus then begins to deal with her issue and pain. As she debates with Him about drawing the physical water from the well, He asks her to call for her husband. She tells Him that she doesn't have one. Jesus then addresses her adultery. He says in John 4:18 -

- "For you have had five husbands, and the one you now have is not your husband. What you have said is true."

Maybe you are like this woman and you have been in a lot of failed relationships. When I say this I am not just referring to physical relationships but you may have had multiple idols filling your life in the place of Jesus. Forget the reasons why you have been in these situations, but understand that Jesus has come to deliver you. He told the woman that an hour was coming when the true worshipers would worship the Father in spirit and in truth and that the Father was looking for these types of worshipers.

I want you to know that the Father is looking at you to be a true worshiper. Remember that worship is not just singing and dancing and the lifting of your hands physically. Worship encompasses a lifestyle of faithfulness to Jesus Christ. Loving Him with everything you have and giving Him the ultimate seat in your heart. The Samaritan woman's response is what is most critical. The Bible says in John 4:28- 30 the following:

- "So the woman left her water jar and went away into town and said to the people, "Come, see a man who told me all that I ever did. Can this be the Christ?"

58

The Samaritan woman had become full of living water so she no longer needed a physical filling. This was shown by her leaving her water pot behind. Relationships with the various men of her life would no longer hold her captive in adultery. She was able to run swiftly and share her message of deliverance to her community.

This is what the call is about. You can be delivered of any idol that is holding you back and receive the love of Jesus. He will empower you to share the good news. I was able to experience the same freedom. I say to you today to leave your water pot right where it is. Run swiftly when you receive the love of God and share what He has done in your life.

You have been called to a life long journey with God. When you walk with Jesus you find real significance to your life. Acts 13:47 says this:

- "For so the Lord has commanded us, saying, 'I have made you a light for the Gentiles, that you may bring salvation to the ends of the earth.'"

Just like the Samaritan woman you have become a light to the world, to help bring salvation to the ends of the earth in Jesus Christ. You no longer have to look for significance in people or idols. God provides the greatest significance we could ever feel.

You no longer have to look for self-worth. The Bible states in 1 John 4:10 the reason why in the following verse:

- This is real love—not that we loved God, but that he loved us and sent his Son as a sacrifice to take away our sins." (*New Living Translation*, 2008)

God values us beyond our imagination. We do not have to bow down to idols in order to gain self-worth. One area of concern that I pose once you have gotten to a new place in God is complacency and potential compromise.

The Old Testament is full of examples of people who had one foot in and one foot out regarding their relationship with God. This is known as mixed worship. In the next chapter I will highlight how mixing the worship of God and of other idols came into the kingdom and how it's being duplicated today. Don't bow!

Don't Bow
Standing against the Idols of Our Generation

Chapter Seven Review

- God is asking you, "Why are you here?" The current place of your compromise.
- Like the Samaritan woman, you may have experienced failed relationships, disappointment, and pain but Jesus provides a living fulfillment that will last forever.
- When Jesus fills you up, we are empowered to share the good news with others.
- As a light to darkness, you have significance.
- You no longer have to look for self-worth. The fact Jesus died for you shows how much he values you!

Chapter Seven Reflection

- What failed relationships or expectations pushed you into idol worship? Now that you recognize these things, know that Jesus is the one who provides true fulfillment. Just like the Samaritan woman he can heal you of your pain and empower you to share of his goodness to a generation. You are called!
- Now that you understand the call that Jesus has on your life, say the following prayer: "Lord Jesus, I accept the call you have placed upon my life. The Samaritan woman had issues but you healed her. God I thank you for healing me as well and empowering me in this call. Jesus, give me boldness to share your good news with my family and friends. In Jesus name, Amen."

Don't Bow
Standing against the Idols of Our Generation

8

Mixed Worship

Some things are just not meant to be together. We all know the 4th grade experiment that encompasses a bowl of water and the mixing of oil. It doesn't work out so well. Some foods would be absolutely horrible together. Nothing could be worse than mixing the purity of worship to Jesus Christ and idols. Unfortunately, the scripture is chalk full of situations in which God's chosen people, the Israelites, committed this egregious act.

God in His meeting with Moses in the book of Exodus began to instruct him regarding the interaction with idols. He knew that mixed worship would become a major issue with His nation. In Exodus 34:10 it says:

- "The LORD replied, "Listen, I am making a covenant with you in the presence of all your people. I will perform miracles that have never been performed anywhere in all the earth or in any nation. And all the people around you will see the power of the LORD— the awesome power I will display for you." (*New Living Translation*, 2008)

What a promise! I would suggest that God is still looking to do wonders among His people. We too as New

Testament believers have been grafted into the covenant and receive the same blessing as the seed of Abraham. He wants to make the church, the body of Christ, a light to the world so that people might know Jesus and all His glory. In order to flow in this promise there are conditions all pertaining to idol worship.

First, God instructs us to obey Him. If we listen to His voice and follow His command He will drive out all of our enemies that are waiting to oppose us in our promise land. You must understand that the place you are trying to get to, whether it is a place of success in your class, whether it is being the first in your family to graduate from college, maybe its finding an amazing job, there will always be enemies to come against you. The children of Israel had their fair share of enemies. God then gives Moses detailed instructions on how to combat the idols of his generation. They are as follows:

- Don't make a treaty with the enemies in your future or

  they will be a snare to you

- Break down your enemies' altars

- Smash their sacred stones

- Cut down their idol poles

- Do not commit yourselves to relationships that will

  lead to idol worship

God has never desired that His children be passive when dealing with idols. He wants us to be bold and confront them head on. A **treaty** is any agreement or compact. It usually deals with a formal agreement between two or more states in reference to peace, alliance, commerce or other international relations.

Don't partner up with an idol for peace. The enemy is not planning on being peaceful to you. He would like to do nothing more than to rob you of your peace and let the idols of our generation cause havoc in your life. Do not align yourself with an idol because they have no sustaining power. Money is material, clothes are material, cars are material, aligning yourself with the idols of our generation can lead to nothing but emptiness after all the flashy stuff goes away. Do not participate in idolatry for money. This is where many in the music industry as previously stated have gone wrong. Lots of artists are literally selling their souls to make millions. The Lord then instructs Moses that the children of Israel are to break down the enemies altars. One way to break down something is to continually chip away at it. Speak out young people. You cannot be silent any longer when you are faced with idols every day.

Many of the idols of our generation are funded with our own dollars. When you go to that famous artist's concert you are supporting their altar. Don't be a voiceless worshiper which is someone that does not audibly praise an idol but through your action worship just as hard as a person shouting to the roof tops. He then goes on to say smash their sacred stones. These pillars were regarded as sacred to the people that worshiped idols. As I stated in the previous chapters rip up every pornographic magazine, delete every image and video that glorifies idol worship.

The Lord then tells Moses that they must cut down their Asherah poles. These images and poles were set up for a historic Canaanite goddess that represented fortune, happiness, and sexual activity. This is exactly what the world wants you to desire, a life full of fortune and happiness and sexual activity but no true fulfillment and joy. God wants you to break down these false senses of self-worth and find your worth in Jesus Christ!

64

He lastly tells Moses not to marry within the tribes of their enemies. This instruction reminds me of what Paul said in 2 Corinthians 6:14 -

- "Don't team up with those who are unbelievers. How can righteousness be a partner with wickedness? How can light live with darkness?" (*New Living Translation*, 2008)

So within church circles, especially young people this comes up all the time. There is a very good reason why God would not want you to engage in activity with individuals who worship the idols of our generation. For one reason the more you are around someone the greater influence they have on your life. Anyone who thinks differently is fooling themselves.

Instead of using the phrase "team up", the King James Version and other translations use the word yoke when describing unequally balanced relationships. A yoke was an instrument that was placed around the neck of two animals as they plowed the farming fields. The imagery that Paul is using is that of two different sized animals like an Ox and a Donkey trying to work together to accomplish a goal. You have specific goals in your life, and a God designed destiny. Some people are not meant to walk along side you because they're not designed to help you stay on the straight and narrow path. In no place is this more evident than in high school. Relationships in this age bracket barely last more than a couple months. Young teenage boys and girls go through tremendous heartache over a failed relationship because they were never equally yoked with the individual they were dating.

Another area where mixed worship is shown in the scriptures is with King Solomon. David's son, Solomon, was thought to be one of the wisest kings in all of Israel's history. He married many wives and received many concubines. All though he was looking to form peace with the nations in which he received wives, it went against the desire of the Lord. He allowed his wives to order the building of tabernacles and edifices of pagan gods. This type of idol worship polluted the kingdom. We are seeing some of the same pollution within the church today. Many in our generation are listening to both Christian/Gospel and Secular music as if there is no issue with the blending worship styles. This area of compromise breaks the heart of God because He knows that worship literally brings you into His presence.

When we listen to or interact with idol worship we drown out the presence of God. When we remove God's presence we eliminate true joy. When we take away joy we lose strength. When our strength is gone so is the desire to fight. The Christian today has to be willing to stand for righteousness. We must stand on the power of God's word.

The revelation that God gave to me regarding mixed worship, is that our generation lives two separate lives. One life is the "church life". This is when a young person attends church on Sundays, Bible study on Wednesdays, and youth outings on Friday and appears committed. This person has an appearance of faithfulness through a busy church life and believes the core of the Bible but hasn't tapped into a deep intimate relationship with Jesus. This person knows the church language and behavioral trends, the popular Gospel artists and preachers, but doesn't fully know the character, ways, and mission of Jesus.

The other life is the "life of compromise". This is the person that is not convicted by secular music or movies that have controversial scenes. This is the person that tries to convince their peers that their favorite artist is saved because they acknowledged God at the award show. This person has become comfortable in sin and totally separates their interactions in the world from that of the church. This is mixed worship.

The prior generation may have some responsibility as to why our generation is in this current predicament. I will preface this by saying the prior generation did amazing things to advance the kingdom of God. If it wasn't for my mother's guidance and my grandmother's prayers I would not be where I am today. Still that generation stood upon their perception of holiness.

This form of holiness had a backlash to it. There were elements of self-righteousness that brought hurt to young people in churches across America. The focus was on the length of the skirt and the type of haircut youth had, and the amount of makeup on their faces. Somewhere lost in this was the inner heart and what was stored inside it. The Bible says in Samuel 16:7 the following:

- "But the Lord said to Samuel, Do not look on his appearance or on the height of his stature, because I have rejected Him. For the Lord sees not as man sees: man looks on the outward appearance, but the Lord looks on the heart."

Now we as a generation have flowed to the opposite end of the spectrum. We have tried to be the antithesis of what was portrayed a few decades ago. We purposefully dress a certain way, we wear certain hairstyles, and dress in makeup to prove that one can be dedicated to a relationship with Jesus and look a certain way and not be off. This is still the wrong premise. God has never been concerned with the outward appearance but has always cared about the content of our hearts. What God is looking for are authentic worshipers who are not mixing the kingdom of God with darkness.

For many of your peers that you interact with on a daily basis, you may be the only example of Jesus they will ever come across. We have a responsibility to represent Him well. A whole generation is looking to you to decide whether or not Christianity is worth it.

So yes, what you listen to, what you watch, what you wear, what you say could potentially bring someone into contact with a savior. Will you be a part of the solution or add to the problem? Make the choice to not compromise and mix your worship. Don't Bow!

Don't Bow
Standing against the Idols of Our Generation

Chapter Eight Review

- When you are in covenant with God, He will do wonders in your life that will be visible by your enemies.

- God does not want you to be passive but desires that you confront the idols that are challenging you head on.

- Young people are living two lives. The "church life" and the "life of compromise". This is literally mixed worship.

- God is not concerned about the outward appearance but is concerned with the content of your heart.

- Mixing worship does matter. What you listen to, watch, and how you act can impact someone looking at your life. Be a reflection of Jesus.

Chapter Eight Reflection

- Mixed worship can be confusing. Not only does it hinder you from being totally free from idol influence but it can keep others from reaching Christ.

- Write down a few things that you believe constitute as mixed worship. Once you identify them say this prayer: "Lord Jesus, I submit these things that are holding back my worship. I desire to worship you in spirit and in truth and I understand my life is a testimony for others to see. I pray that my worship is pure and that it brings my friends and family closer to you. In Jesus name, Amen."

Don't Bow
Standing against the Idols of Our Generation

9

Last Day Outpour

There is no question that we are living in a troubling time. The moral compass is pointed in a downward direction for our nation. The next generation is faced with great opposition. Throughout this text I have highlighted the images and idols that are prevalent in today's society. The Bible has been strong in its stance against idol worship and it has also informed us on what is coming down the road. The prophet Joel spoke about a future outpouring of the Holy Spirit that would occur in the lives of young men and women. He states in Joel 2:28 -

- "And it shall come to pass afterward, that I will pour out my Spirit on all flesh; your sons and your daughters shall prophesy, your old men shall dream dreams, and your young men shall see visions."

What an awesome prophetic expectation for our generation. God is planning to pour out His Spirit to empower young men and women with the ability to speak to dead things and see them come back to life. The Lord desires to give a clear vision to the next generation. In the last days young people will see the light at the end of the tunnel and refuse to be influenced by the darkness of idols.

Many young people have heard this word preached at their churches, at youth retreats, and even on many of the Gospel television networks but are not sure how this will truly happen. The requirement is a full turning away or repentance of the sins that the people had committed toward God. You may be asking yourself what sins? What have I personally done? Young people have bowed down to the modern day idols and have desired their ways more than the ways of God. Some may have openly participated in the commonly known sins that plague teenagers across the country; others may have been ignorant because no one ever shared with them what was wrong with their activity.

Unfortunately, ignorance is not an excuse. This is why I am writing this book. It is important that someone stands up on the wall of our cities, our states, and our nation and declare the righteousness of God. We must be a sounding board for our youth and let them know they have a purpose and destiny. Have I been perfect throughout my life? By no means, Jesus was the only one to do that. Still, that doesn't mean that I shouldn't flow in the conviction of the Holy Spirit to expose the plan of the enemy, especially if it has been test run in my own life.

When a nation turns back to God great and mighty things will happen. The Lord exclaims in the book of Joel to turn back to Him with all your heart, with fasting, with weeping, and with mourning. God is calling for a radical response to the sin of our nation. Jesus wants us to turn to Him with everything. The heart is literally the seat of our emotion. It is the place where true intentions dwell. With every bit of honesty regarding our life, God wants us to turn and give that to Him. He wants us to fast. This is a challenging but necessary area for me and many in our generation. This is primarily due to not knowing what constitutes true fasting. More than just denying the flesh, fasting is engaging God. We must couple denying the delicacies of life which can be food and or entertainment with time in God's presence.

This is what Jesus wants. From acknowledging the idols that are in your life, to understanding how they function in society. Getting a full picture of what the heart void entails and how to rid yourself of the idol virus, it is all in preparation of the call that God has on your life and the outpouring of His Spirit on you. What is encouraging is God's decision to empower the youth in this great move. This shouldn't be a surprise. God has started many great movements with young people. When we look at the life of David we see how God desired to anoint him when he was ready to move in a new way within the nation of Israel. 1 Samuel 16:11-12 says:

• Then Samuel said to Jesse, "Are all your sons here?" And he said, "There remains yet the youngest, but behold, he is keeping the sheep." And Samuel said to Jesse, "Send and get him, for we will not sit down till he comes here." And he sent and brought him in. Now he was ruddy and had beautiful eyes and was handsome. And the LORD said, "Arise, anoint him, for this is he."

The Bible then records that Samuel took the horn of oil and anointed David among his brothers. The Spirit of the Lord rested upon David from that day forward. Jesus is looking to do the same thing today for our youth. He wants to anoint us with his Spirit in this last day outpour.

Gideon was another young man in the Bible that was anointed by the Spirit of God. With three hundred men Gideon led a charge against Israel's enemies and defeated them. The prophet Jeremiah as previously stated was anointed to be a prophet of God and speak a message of repentance to the nation. He did so despite the consensus understanding of what an appropriate age was to serve in that capacity. These are just a few examples of how God desires to use young people to lead the charge back to His presence.

God wants to use you! Yes, his plan is for young people across America and in the world to stand up for His name, refusing to bow down to idols, to be used as mouthpieces to prophesy hope to a lost generation.

God doesn't want to just pour out His Spirit on young people who preach his Gospel but He wants to do this in every arena that our youth are in. He desires to empower young people in their high schools that can shift a culture by their witness and by leading prayer and bible clubs. He wants to challenge athletes to live for Jesus and share their testimony with those who do not know the Lord in the locker room. God wants to strengthen college students to start prayer movements and help bring the presence of God to their campuses. The Lord wants more for you than the false fulfillment you have currently been receiving from idol worship. Will you make a decision today to turn from the destructive path that our modern day idols have led us down? If so, take the Don't Bow pledge.

Don't Bow
Standing against the Idols of Our Generation

Chapter Nine Review

- We are living in tough times but we are also at the beginning of a great outpour.
- God is pouring his Spirit upon our generation and we will be gifted to prophesy the word of the Lord.
- The pre-requisite of this outpour is repentance, a true turning away of our sins. As a generation we must admit our short-comings to the Lord and sincerely seek his face.
- God uses youth whenever he gets ready to do a great move within a nation.
- God gives you his Spirit to live a saved life and to be empowered to influence others in your school, job, sports team, etc.

Chapter Nine Reflection

- God has already been filling young people across the globe. If you want to be empowered as the Bible says, repentance is a must. It is a sincere heartfelt confession and turning away from idol worship. Take the action today to be filled with God's power!
- Say the following prayer regarding the final outpour: "Lord Jesus, I pray that you fill me with your Spirit and that you start a movement with me, in this nation to impact my place of influence. I pray that everyone I come across will experience your love. In Jesus name, Amen."

Don't Bow
Standing against the Idols of Our Generation

10

The Don't Bow Pledge

In this chapter we want to encourage high school and college students to take the "Don't Bow Pledge". Before we give information on the pledge, perhaps you have never accepted Jesus Christ as your Lord and savior. If not you can commit to Him by expressing your understanding of His sacrifice. Jesus Christ died for your sins so that you wouldn't have to. He paid the ultimate price and because of that we can reap eternal life.

A fellow teacher in Jesus's day was curious about this salvation process and so he came to Him at night time to ask for himself. He wanted to know how a man could be born again. Jesus responded by saying a man must be born of both water and spirit (John 3:5). If you want to take that next step in your walk with Jesus and experience the new birth, please have a real conversation with the Lord right now. Confess to Him your sins and that you believe He is the Son of God. That He died, was buried, and was resurrected.

It's amazing to speak something out in the open that you believe in your heart. Now that you have confessed, let your actions couple with your words. Go to your local church and let your youth or senior pastor know that you are ready to take the next step in relationship with Jesus via water and spirit baptism. They will walk you through these steps with great care and guidance. If you do not have a local church then please email us at info@dontbowthebook.com and we may be able to connect you with a strong Bible believing church. In addition, share with your parents or other family members that care for you, what you have chosen to do. They will be a great support to you moving forward in this faith journey.

Now in regards to the Don't Bow Pledge it encompasses a commitment statement. At the end of the day what you commit to Jesus Christ is what matters but this is just a vehicle to help you get there. In order to complete the pledge please visit www.dontbowthebook.com and complete the form online.

I **(your name)** pledge to not bow down to the images and idols that are a part of my generation. I understand the challenge of taking a righteous stand and forsaking the ways of the world but regardless I commit to giving my all to the cause of Jesus Christ. I **(your name)** will monitor my social media accounts and with honesty delete anything that could hold me back in idol worship. I **(your name)** will be attentive to the music and entertainment I expose myself to and with speed turn away from anything that aims to hinder my progress.

I **(your name)** pray to be a leader of my generation and to be a light to others who may be bound by the images and idols of our day. I **(your name)** take this Don't Bow Pledge in faith knowing that Jesus Christ is my strength.

In Jesus Name,

Amen

If you have completed the don't bow pledge please let us know so that we can connect and continue to pray with you. I want each and every reader to know that God loves you and wants the best for you. He doesn't want you to be influenced by images and idols but would rather you be the one to help transform a generation. If you hear this clarion call, the sound of a messenger on the wall, I leave you with this exhortation. Don't Bow!

ABOUT THE AUTHOR

The journey with God has been an interesting one for Pastor DeMarquis Battle. While attending Valparaiso University and playing Division 1-AA football, Pastor Battle experienced many ups and downs. During this time of isolation, God met him in a very profound way. It was during that time God first touched Pastor Battle's heart to reach the lost through the preaching of the Gospel.

During spring break in 2006, he visited a church on the campus of Michigan State University in East Lansing, Michigan while visiting his older sister. It was this event that would change his life forever. While visiting that church, Pastor Battle would experience the outpouring of God's presence and weekly revival that was happening there under the ministry of Pastor Sean Holland. Pastor Battle knew that God was leading him to this place to be planted as a servant to the lost in that region. Pastor Battle would leave everything behind to become a member of the Epicenter of Worship Church and serves there to this day.

Pastor Battle has served faithfully as a Campus Evangelist and currently serves as an Associate Pastor at the Epicenter of Worship Church in Lansing, MI. Pastor Battle holds a Bachelor of Arts degree in Multidisciplinary Studies from Siena Heights University, a Master of Arts degree in Ministry Studies from Grace College & Seminary, and a Master of Arts degree in Bible & Theology from Lincoln Christian University. Pastor Battle is married to his best friend who he has known since the 7th grade, Raynika Battle, and they have a 2 year old son named Justus Benjamin Battle. Pastor Battle desires to see a generation rise up and walk in their purpose making known the power and saving grace of Jesus Christ.

Contact Information:

P.O. Box 81189
Lansing, MI 48908

Email: info@battleleadershipgroup.com

Social Media:
www.facebook.com/dontbowthebook
www.youtube.com/dontbowthebook
www.twitter.com/dontbowthebook
www.twitter.com/ministerbattle
www.twitter.com/BattleLeaderGrp

Twitter hash tags (#):
#dontbow
#dontbowthebook
#idols
#images

Websites:
www.battleleadershipgroup.com

References:

[1] LifeWay research finds reasons 18-to-22 year-olds drop out of church. (2007). Retrieved August 17, 2013, from http://www.lifeway.com/Article/LifeWay-Research-finds-reasons-18-to-22-year-olds-drop-out-of-church

[2] Drug facts- prescription drugs. (2013). Retrieved August 17, 2013, from http://teens.drugabuse.gov/drug-facts/prescription-drugs

[3] Adolescent and school health. (2007). Retrieved August 22, 2013, from http://www.cdc.gov/healthyyouth/sexualbehaviors/srh.htm

[4] MDMA-ecstasy or molly. (2013). Retrieved August 17, 2013, from http://teens.drugabuse.gov/drug-facts/mdma-ecstasy-or-molly

www.ingramcontent.com/pod-product-compliance
Lightning Source LLC
Chambersburg PA
CBHW071418040426
42445CB00012BA/1207